Surviving Suicide

One Mother's Journey to Acceptance After Her Son's Death

Found in Jason's images, April 10, 2016

Surviving Suicide
One Mother's Journey to Acceptance After
Her Son's Death

Victoria Polmatier

Copyright © 2017 by Victoria Polmatier

All rights reserved. No part of this book may be reproduced in any form or by any electronic or mechanical means, except in the case of brief quotations with proper reference embodied in articles or reviews, without written permission from its author.

Mystic Haven Press
PO Box 874102
Vancouver, WA 98687
www.mystichavenpress.com

Edited by: Kerri Miller
Cover design by: Victoria Polmatier

All images used by permission and labeled as to the photographer

ISBN 978-0-9993445-0-7
ISBN 978-0-9993445-1-4 (ebook)
ISBN 978-0-9993445-2-1 (Kindle)

Library of Congress Control Number: 2017914373

All quotations remain the intellectual property of their respective originators. All use of quotations is done under the fair use copyright principle.

Dedication

In loving memory of my son
Jason.

I dedicate this book to my husband.
You have shared this journey
and been my rock throughout.

I want to thank my family.
You have supported me and this project
with your time and your love.

Contents

I Will Always Love You	x
Prologue	12
Farewell	14
The Man of the Beautiful Mask	16
Start Writing Again	18
Black Hole of Despair	20
I've Learned, Day 11	22
No Tears	23
Life Goes On	24
Full Circle	26
Unexpected Tears	28
I've Learned, Day 23	29
The Tornado Has Ended	30
Surrender	32
My Birthday	35
Grief's Tears	36
Breadcrumbs	38
I've Learned, Day 43	40
Dark Circles	41
The Spider Runs Round and Round	42
Inspirations in a Bottle	44
What If I Love Again	48
Who You Are	50
Breakfast Remembered	51

Air Thick with Grief	52
Family, Part 1	54
Family, Part 2	56
Party Night	58
This Crazy Maze	60
I've Learned, Day 83	61
The Loss of My Son	64
Ebb and Flow	65
Grief's Anger	67
What I Know	70
I Could Feel It	72
Two Worlds	74
Wandering	76
Winter	78
Holidays	80
Winter Cold	82
Memories	83
One Step At A Time	84
Crossing A Line	86
Ice Storm	88
Another Year	89
An Evening of Remembrance	92
Spring's Stirring	96
Your Presence	98
The Spaces Between	100

The Darkness Surrounds Me	102
Returning to the Light	104
A Gathering of Family	106
Happy Birthday	108
Spring Forth	110
Grief Sucks	111
A Window in Time	113
Dispelling the Energy	115
His Civic Nature	116
Standing in the Midst	118
What Does Today Hold	120
No Do-Overs	122
Breaking Down Barriers	124
The Man Behind the Beautiful Mask	126
Good Mom?	128
Ponderings on Life Without Jason	130
A Nighttime Visit	131
This Roller Coaster Called Grief	132
Driving Down the Road	134
Warm Day Memories	136
Mother's Day, Part 1	138
Mother's Day, Part 2	139
Mother's Day, Part 3	140
Mr. Kitty's Freedom	142
He Knew	144

Moving Forward	146
Black and White and Tuna Sandwiches	148
Choice Points	150
A Frame of Photos	152
Coming Home	154
Almost a Year	156
Some Things	158
In a Different Reality	159
I Was a Tormented Soul	160
Epilogue	162
Author Bio	169

I Will Always Love You
February 27, 2016

I see a beautiful soul
swimming alone in the dark.
You can reach out to me
when you know you're drowning.
I'm terrified when I see
that look in your eyes of hovering
on the abyss of darkness.
I long to see contentment
and peace in your eyes
to celebrate your todays
without fear for tomorrow.
I want to know you're okay.
When you don't think you
can hold on one more day
I love you, and I see you.
I love you in your dark
and in your light.
I love you
no matter the cost.

Photo by Jason

Prologue

My son Jason took his life sometime between the evening of July 23 and the afternoon of July 24, 2016. I can't honestly say I was surprised: I had known for a while that it was a possibility. In the months before his death, he had made a series of bad decisions and gotten himself into trouble. Then he lost his job of ten years.

In conversations with the family, everyone would ask the same question: "Will he be okay?" He had struggled with depression for years and made three previous attempts to take his life. Between attempts, however, he'd be positive and upbeat.

Jason was a man who lived behind a beautiful mask. He was smart, well-dressed, a contributor to work and society at large. He had a wicked sense of humor and loved to pull pranks on his friends and co-workers. The persona he presented to the world was of a man in control of his life.

But in the quiet of his mind, he suffered deeply. In reviewing his personal effects, I found he had a high degree of self-loathing. He struggled with relationships and finances and feeling effective in his personal life. This internal suffering led him down a dark path.

An incredibly private individual, Jason normally stayed in contact with friends and family but kept his mask securely in place. We never knew he was back in that dark place until we'd get the terrifying call that he'd tried to end his life.

This time had been different. We knew he was in trouble and worried he would attempt suicide again. He moved in with us for support. Several times a week he went to his apartment to start cleaning it out.

On Saturday, July 23rd Jason called to say he was going to stay at his apartment because he wanted to visit with a friend. The next morning he was supposed to join us on a shopping trip for a new laptop. But he didn't show up. He didn't return phone calls or texts. So we went to look for him. Unfortunately, concern and vigilance had made no difference. His struggle was over.

Victoria Polmatier
March 4, 2017

Farewell
July 25, 2016

The end.
The story is over.
No more worry
no more angst.
I'm sorry that
you couldn't find another way
that life got so hard
that you couldn't see beyond tomorrow.
I'm sorry to let you go.
I'll miss your sense of humor
your playful spirit
your tender soul
your amazing photos
watching you finish our garden path.
I'll miss you, my son.
I'm proud to have been your mom.
I'm proud of the man you were.
I'd take another day of worry
just to see your smiling face again.
I'd take a lifetime of struggles
if only that would bring you back home.
But you lie there lifeless,
nothing more to be done now.
We'll have to find a way through
the pain and the darkness.
I have moments —
I know I'll think of you
in every smiling face

of a tender flower.
I'll think of you
when I walk up that pathway.
Your pots of flowers will stand
for the bright shining soul
I know you were.
You've burned a hole
in my heart
that will last forever.
Bright blessings and farewell
my beautiful son.

The Man of the Beautiful Mask

In the days after Jason's death, his friends, family, and co-workers shared the following thoughts on his Facebook wall.

I'll miss his smile, his giggle, his kindness
his knack for seeing the beauty everywhere.
I'll miss the numerous belly-hurting
tears-running-down our faces laughs.
I'll miss our candid conversations
his passion for helping the community
politics, photography
plants and flowers, Mr. Kitty.
Truly one of the good guys.
Genuinely kind.
No questions asked.
No judgment.
Funny, quick to smile, teasing.
Smart, handsome, helpful, kind
a hard worker, a real friend.
Genuine.
He loved a good prank
had a happy heart, even when he was down
could always find a brighter side.
His smile lit up the entire room.
He touched the lives of many people.
An amazing man.
It's hard to imagine life without
his laughter, goofiness and sparkle.
He truly made me a better person.

A sweet and loving friend
intelligent, informed
creative,
genius,
dedication.
One of a kind.

Photo by Matthew Bernard Bentson-Royal

Start Writing Again
August 2, 2016

My mom said
start writing again.
I know she's right.
Writing helps me
clear my mind
bring emotions
to the surface
and release them.
But now I feel
as if I'm drowning.
Jason's death
has drained the light
out of my life.
I put one foot
in front of the other
but there's this weight
I drag behind me
makes everything
take twice as long
as it did before —
before Jason
solved his darkness
by ending his life.
I suppose I'm lucky
I learned in the weeks
before his death
what haunted him.
I don't have to wonder

or wish I'd done something
more, different, better.
But it opens
a whole other line
of inquiry
inside my mind
that leads nowhere;
I'll never have answers.
Instead, I grieve
with a world of others
touched by the beauty
of Jason —
his humor and wit
his gentle spirit
his black and white thinking
his passion for excellence.
What's left in his place —
an emptiness, a void.
The world is dimmer than before
the colors of the trees and flowers
he loved so much — now dull and lifeless.
And so, I wander, moment to moment
waiting for a peace so long in coming.

Black Hole of Despair
August 3, 2016

swirling
black hole
of despair
unable to breathe
weight
dragging me down
down
down
can't reach out
can't speak
frozen in time

explosion
a fit of rage
words spewed
anger flying
intake of breath
stopping
in my tracks

release
sudden washing
of tears
rolling down my cheeks
clearing away the debris
I can breathe again
for now, anyway
until the next wave

comes crashing over
drowning me
in grief

Photo by Jason

I've Learned, Day 11
August 4, 2016

I've learned
you never really understand
the life-sucking effects
of grief
until you've been there.

I've learned
a good day
doesn't necessarily mean
you'll have another
anytime soon.

I've learned
life goes on
the good and the bad.
Grief doesn't mean
you get a pass.

I've learned
about the time you think
you've mapped where grief resides
it will peek out
when you least expect it
take you by the throat
and have its way with you.

No Tears
August 7, 2016

no tears today
just this intense
tightness in my chest
tears
buried deep in my being
no release
just this holding tight
waiting
unknowing
we'll have to see

Life Goes On
August 7, 2016

Once again, I'm not sleeping.
Wandering through my computer
I found this picture of Jason
the evening before he took his life
an action that changed my life
and our family, forever.
I wish I'd known when we sat
around that campfire
what he was contemplating.
I remember he seemed different.
He didn't play in the fire
which was his normal antic.
He just sat and watched
one last time together
a silent goodbye.

Two weeks have passed
and from the outside —
the appearance of normalcy.
The tears have stopped, mostly —
at least when I'm among others.
I find myself laughing
at a joke or a funny post
enjoying the company of friends
excited about our nuptials
and finally saying, "I do."
But all the time
I carry this pain in my heart

a tightness in my chest
so hard to breathe
no appetite
nauseous
all inner things
that none can see or hear.
It's strange to enjoy life
while my heart is hurting.
But that appears to be
the way of my life now.
And really
I have no other choice.

Photo by Victoria

Full Circle
August 11, 2016

We've come full circle
you and I.
You started as
an embryo
in my womb.
You grew into
a beautiful baby
I held in my arms.
As a small boy
I remember you swinging
eyes far away
deep in thought.
You became
a thoughtful young man
with wit and humor
as your sword.

Now you are tucked
safe in my heart
where I'll hold you
for eternity.

Photo by Jason's father, of Jason and Victoria

Unexpected Tears
August 13, 2016

Standing in the store
helping my husband-to-be
select his wedding clothes.
He steps out
in a new outfit:
it's perfect.
My heart fills with love.
He turns to walk back in
the dressing room
and the awareness
crashes in.
He won't be there.
My son.
Our son won't be at our wedding.
Tears begin to flow
quietly down my cheeks.
Nothing to do
but wait for mourning
to subside
and turn my attention
back to the love I feel.

I've Learned, Day 23
August 16, 2016

I've learned
grief is a physical weight
you carry in your heart.
You learn to endure it.
But there will be times
when the weight's unbearable
like it was in the beginning.

I've learned
just when you think you've faced
all there is to face
something comes along
and thrusts you back
into grief again.

The Tornado Has Ended
August 24, 2016

The tornado has ended.
Life is finally still.
I sit amidst the ruins
with hints of new life.
But the ruins—
I can't get beyond the ruins.
Jason took his life
a month ago today.
Since then
my mom's had major surgery
and I got married.
It's been thirty days today
since my world turned upside down.
I should be celebrating, dammit!
After fourteen years together
Tom and I got married!
I look at him and feel
such love and tenderness.
But all the time
my heart hurts.
How do I turn this around?
How do I find LIFE again?
I've crossed a raging river and
don't recognize the landscape.
It's not the comfortable beauty of home.
It's simply a foreign land.
There are days I think
I can manage the grief

but the rest of the time
I struggle to find a smile.
My old way of being in the world
seems gone
I'm floating from day to day
with no direction.
When the family leaves this weekend
what will fill my days?
Projects won't heal this brokenness.
This will be a long journey
with no clear pathway
and no clear ending.
Put one foot in front of the other
do what's in front of me to do
and wait for the day
when this great gaping hole
in my heart heals
and only scars remain.

Surrender
August 30, 2016

I'm surrendering
to the death of my son.
It's been five weeks now.
We've taken every turn
to access his world.

It's ironic
in the "olden" days
before electronics
a person's affairs
would be in a box
or file cabinet.
Papers could be
accessed
sorted
read.
Pictures could be
viewed
appreciated
remembered.

Now we have this
huge world
held in the cloud
stored on computers
laptops, cell phones.
But there's a catch.
We have security

to protect us
and it can mean
limited access
by our loved ones
when we're gone.

So we've tossed and turned
become amateur hackers
into the world
that was my son's.
We've had successes.
We have his pictures
lovely photography
that inspired many.
The rest
we'll release.
Anything important
will show up in
the snail mail.

So today,
I surrender —
I let go.
I have my memories.
Fighting the
electronic world
won't bring my son back.
What's there is lost
in the mists of the cloud.
He's gone.
That's it.

It's time to accept
and move on.
Damn, it's hard.

Photo by Jason

My Birthday
September 2016

Today's my 58th birthday
and I've spent most of the day
with tears rolling down my cheeks.
You'd think that I was ungrateful
but I am incredibly blessed.
I have a wonderful husband
my mate of fourteen years.
I have a beautiful home
surrounded by tall trees.
I have a loving mother
and an awesome daughter
and lots of amazing family
friends, an abundant life.
But I have this hole in my heart.
Likely, because it's my birthday
I feel Jason's presence
and it makes me cry
cry for the life lost
for the possibilities unrealized.
This too shall pass
life happens that way.
In time
the hole he's left in my heart
will become a container
overflowing with love.

Grief's Tears
September 2016

Another day
another hangover.
It seemed like a promising idea
when I started last night—
drink margaritas
extinguish the pain
of a birthday and no son.
Now
I sit frozen
emotions right back
at the surface.
In truth
I can't make this
go away
no matter
how hard I try
how much I drink
how many salty tears I cry.
It's here to stay—
the pain
the anguish
the grief.
It seems that they
will be my forever friends.
Some say this will pass
but I'm not certain.
The tears won't stop.
They sit

poised and ready to flow
at will.
Not mine, but some
unnamable force
that causes them to cascade
down my cheeks
until I'm sobbing
no end in sight.
Eventually
they clear
and I am silent
until the next free-fall
into the hell
that is grief.

Breadcrumbs
September 3, 2016

it's been a week of highs and lows
revelations, disbelief
coming to terms
all the while continuing to love

there is no easy way to learn
about the inner workings of
a depressed man who took his life
leaving a trail of breadcrumbs to
the inner world he couldn't live with

the man with the beautiful mask
is being unmasked

Photo by Jason

I've Learned, Day 43
September 5, 2016

I've learned
it simply is.
Like there's a color
ripped from the rainbow.
And all the crying
and railing I do
won't bring it back.
He's simply gone
and life goes on
with one less color.

Dark Circles
September 8, 2016

Dark circles
Under the eyes
Tell the story
Of pain and lies.

Photo by Jason

The Spider Runs Round and Round
September 19, 2016

exploding emotions
bottled inside
antsy
but can't move
the spider runs
round and round
the monitor
i am blocked
it's that simple
but not simple at all
confusion in my mind
crazy in my head
vibrations in my body
trying to connect
with what's at the bottom
what's making me feel CRAZY?
another layer of letting go
or refusal to let go
holding on for dear life
to a life that no longer exists
tears roll
i should have held him more
repeats in my head
a lost soul
rambling in this world
saw nowhere to turn
allowed the demons
in his head

to devour him whole
images
words
moments
lost in the fog
of what could have been
but will be no more
some days i can move beyond
today i'm buried in the loss
can't breathe
can't let go
i should have held him more
and the spider runs
round and round

Inspirations in a Bottle
September 21, 2016

Today, I gave in, grabbed a bottle of wine and went for a walk around our property. The following snippets came to me as I progressed through the bottle.

There's a whole world of pain
no one talks about
buried deep inside of us
clamoring to get out.
It shows up as drinking and drugging
cutting oneself
giving away our bodies
to be used again and again
seeking a release
that doesn't devour the soul.

If we're just a speck in the universe
a tiny mote in time
why does it sometimes feel
that life contains eternity?

And so today
I ponder the shades of grief
views from the swing set
views from Jason's resting place
views from the ground
such beautiful grass

skin burning

on fire
another hot flash of grief

He has no idea
I emptied a bottle
this afternoon.
"You drive," he says
not knowing I
had no business driving.
But I do.
And here I sit
margarita on top
wondering how we made it home.

Heading to the bottom
is so easy
no resistance
just a steady
march downwards.

All of them
have no idea
what this path
is really like
slowly
descending
to
the end.

I didn't remember writing the last two stanzas. They were there when I went to collect poetry for this book. It was almost as if they came from Jason.

Photo by Jason

Throughout my life I have lived with a tough inner task master. I never quite measure up to my ideas of who I should be or what I should be doing. For me, I've learned to get up and move— ignore those voices in my mind telling me I'm not good enough or I need to do more. Move, do something, make something, don't just sit around. It's kept me sane.

It seems Jason struggled with similar demons. The difference—they got the better of him. He never learned the skill to ignore and move.

There have been times, both in the months leading up to his death and certainly after, where I have had the sense we walk a unified path. Before his death, I felt pain and thought it was my pain. After his death, I realized part of the pain I felt might have been his.

In this bit of poetry, it's as though he's reaching back from the other side. I am still feeling his pain in my grieving.

What If I Love Again
September 27, 2016

What if I love again?
What if I dismantle
the walls I carefully built
to protect my tender heart?
What if I allow others
into my inner sanctum?
What if I love
with every ounce
of my being?
What if my heart
gets broken again?
What if I learn
all I can learn?
Will I be required
to give something back?
Will I give too much
until I break open?
Will I still exist?
Will I survive?
Will I live
to do it again?

Love asks us
to give of ourselves.
Love asks us
to bare our hearts.
Love asks us
to take down walls.

Love asks us to trust—
in the possibility
the beauty
the strength
of the human heart.
So, yes—
I will love
I will give
I will do it all again.

Who You Are
September 30, 2016

Who you truly are
speaks louder
than anything
you can ever do.

Photo by Amber, Jason's sister

Breakfast Remembered
October 3, 2016

I'm making breakfast.
I've thrown together
a few leftovers
from this weekend
to make a scramble.
I realize that it looks
like the scramble I'd get
from the Cup and Saucer
our favorite restaurant
for breakfast in Portland.
The last time I was there
was with Jason.
And the tears
begin to roll.

Air Thick with Grief
October 5, 2016

It's one of those days
when the air
is thick with grief
and tears are close.
It's as though
Jason were
right
here.
Perhaps it was
the morning scare
his Mr. Kitty
nowhere in sight.
A walk around.
Any signs?
Nothing.
Eventually
he strolls in
nonchalant.
But still the air
is thick with grief.
Me —
too weighted down
to write today.

Photo by Jason

Family, Part 1
October 6, 2016

Have I mentioned lately
how important
family is?
We each define it
to our liking.
Blood binds some.
Others form
by a common bond.

In my case
it includes my husband
(still feels strange
to call him that);
my Mom because
we worked so hard
to get so close
and she's not getting
any younger;
my daughter
an amazing woman
though sometimes she forgets;
my son
who is no longer
on this Earth.
But wait, there's more
my husband's sister
and her husband,
my husband's children

and grandchildren —
all my bonus family.
And there have been others.

No matter the form
it's the foundation
for our lives
and sometimes the pattern
for who we become.
Family creates
a protective space
for us to flourish
celebrate together
and hold one another
in grieving loss.
Without family
we are lost and alone.
Cherish your family.

Photo by Amber (Jason's sister), of Amber and Jason

Family, Part 2
October 6, 2016

Family:
parents, siblings, children
grandparents, grandchildren
significant others
that one person
in all the world
who understands YOU.
Family is important.
It's easy to say
hard to practice.
Time is an element
we struggle with
in the Western world.
Time for all those
things we need to do.
Time for the world
of social media.
Time for everything
but seldom family.
Take the time.
Make the plans
and stick to them.
Spend time
quality time
with those you love.

You never know
when tomorrow
won't
come.

Photo by Amber (Jason's sister), Jason & his maternal grandmother

Party Night
October 10, 2016

party night
wasted day
turns in time
to wasted life
makes me hate
myself again
it's a piece
of the answer
as to how
Jason chose
suicide
it's not all
but it's a piece
and today
i feel like crap
my body ill
mind dull
more and more
i'm doing this
pain
grief
find escape
i chose the drink
not even sure
how i got
as far as i did

one drink
at a time
it's how all
of life happens
one
at a time

This Crazy Maze
October 12, 2016

taking care
of busy-ness
little tasks
to clean the mess
drag the mind
use my time
poor excuse
to thwart the muse
cleaning house
like a busy mouse
i'll be glad
to pass this phase
so i can escape
this crazy maze

I've Learned, Day 83
October 15, 2016

I've learned
grief never really leaves
though it does
become less present.
There are days now
when I remember
but I don't cry.
I still ache.
I'm guessing
I will always ache
but life is moving on.

I've learned
some days the grief
will still be overwhelming
tears will come in streams
sometimes brought on
by events
other times just happening.
They may last minutes
or many hours
but eventually
they subside
and a calmness
will take over.

I've learned
that grief can't

be wished away
or chased away
by some mental
strategy.
It's real.
It's here and now.
It's part of the cost
of love.

Photo by Jason

The Loss of My Son
October 15, 2016

The loss of my son
has been among
the hardest journeys
of my life.
It has changed me
at the core.
It has taught me
just how fragile
life can be.
It has taught me
to trust my gut
and to ask
the tough questions.
It's taught me not
to back down
with those I love
and the importance
of connecting.
I am more tender
I am more open
and I cry often.

Ebb and Flow
October 18, 2016

Ebb and flow
cycles
seasons
come and go
rising, falling
life and death.
No one knows
how long the cycle
but the transience
is certain.
In truth we are
the merest point
in an ever-woven
tapestry.
Resistance only
makes it painful.
Let go
feel the breath
feel the cycles.
Cool earth
yields to verdant
green growth
blooms
produces fruit
wilts away
drying, falling
composting
to cool earth.

A new life
grows and changes
if it doesn't
die early
ages, wrinkles
dries out
soon or late
returns
to cool earth.
It's all part
of a cycle
ebb and flow.
Life.

Grief's Anger
October 21, 2016

I knew grief
comes with a
degree of anger.
I assumed
that it would be
anger at you
for taking your life
for leaving us
behind
asking why.
But instead
anger looks like
being pissed off
at my mate
for nothing
stupid stuff
like putting the lid
on the floor
for the dogs to lick.
Anger looks like
my inability
to sit still
or meditate.
Anger looks like
being pissed
at all these people
writing about grief.
I'll admit

some are good
(thanks, Rebecca)
but all too many
have never borne
these depths of grief.
They prescribe
ten handy tips
for letting go
of a job or boyfriend
or other insignificant
grief.
I understand.
I've been there.
I've bemoaned
what I know now
is small stuff.
But the big one.
It's different.
You can't just
let it go.
It's not simple.
And my anger
is boiling over
scalding me
and those around me.
I want to scream
with rage.
I want to beat
on something
anything.
I need an outlet

for this rage
this grief
this pain
wrapped in
helplessness.

What I Know
October 31, 2016

Here's what I know:
Grief is a force
with its energy center
like a hurricane
not simple
like a snow storm
here this week
and gone the next
melted away
only a memory.
You can't debate
or control it.
It comes when it will.
It is as strong
as deep
as gentle
as it desires.
You can't decide
to let it go
and see it out
the back door.
It's not that easy.
You can decide
to go on living
with grief as a
constant companion.
You can decide
you'll let your loved one

hold the pain
that they have caused
but the grief
is unabated.
I don't know how long
it will last.
It's new to me.
I just know
that there are days
it hurts like hell.

I Could Feel It
November 11, 2016

Some days it seems
that Life asks more
than I can give.
I have a habit
of not taking care
of myself
burying pain
and frustration
in alcohol
or sugar
not facing
what I'm feeling.
Jason has been
on my mind
again.
I've been thinking
of his visits
in the last months
of his life.
They got longer.
There was a quality
I couldn't quite
identify.
When he went home
we'd talk about
how he was doing.
I felt uneasy
but couldn't find

a cause for concern.
Now, looking back
I can see —
no, I can feel
what I was missing
at the time.
The clues were there
in front of me
if only I'd
allowed myself
to see them.
I'm trying hard
not to blame
but it's so plain now
I'm straining not
to feel the guilt
but simply to
let go.

Two Worlds
November 18, 2016

I feel as though
I walk between
two worlds
the world before
he took his life
and the world thereafter.
I can almost
pretend for a while
that all is okay.
I can remember
the person he was.
But suddenly
the recognition
of where we are
engulfs me.
The pain comes
crashing back
overwhelming
suffocating
forming a weight
in my chest.
In retrospect
I see the signposts
along the way.
But hindsight can't
undo the past.
At that time
he seemed okay

doing well.
Mental illness
depression
suicide —
they're deceptive
silent assassins
only obvious
when you look back.

Wandering
November 28, 2016

wandering
lost
in the forest
of my mind
glimpses
moments
memories
then the fog
rolls in
dimming vision
leaving me
adrift again
today
i step onto a path
dragging myself
forward
determined
to find my way
out of the forest
of grief
and loss
it's a slow path
one i know
will take many
twists and turns

but i must
drag myself
up and back
into the light

Photo by Jason

Winter
December 6, 2016

Yesterday
we had snow.
It was lovely.
Today it's gone
and in its place
the chilly temps
a biting wind
and the sunshine.
The air feels different.
Winter's here.
The natural world
has settled in
for a winter's rest.
The first freeze of
the year will come
tonight.
It's very odd
to harvest veggies
from the garden
in December.
The freeze tonight
would surely kill them.
With that the garden
joins the winter
slumber.
I feel myself
moving slower
sleeping more

hunkering down.
This year has been
a wild ride
and I'm ready
for a respite.

Holidays
December 13, 2016

My heart is heavy
tears are always
threatening.
I tried ignoring
Christmas, doing
only things
I don't connect with Jason.
Christmas was
his favorite holiday.
He'd start early
with the carols
sometimes in September.
He gave
to families in need
instead of giving
or receiving
with his family.
I'm finally listening
to Christmas music.
It's almost
unbearable
but can't pretend
there is no Christmas.
The fire in
the fireplace
the threat of snow
we rarely get
would all be things

that he'd be thrilled about
adding extra joy
to his Christmas delight.
So in his honor
I wish you
a joyous holiday
regardless of
the way you celebrate
or the joy
or pain
in your heart.

Winter Cold
December 15, 2016

i rage
i try to stay busy
i ache
a deep soul ache
spinning in the winter wind
the cold creeps in my bones
the tears are threatening to make
icicles down my cheeks
this is the winter
of my soul's unraveling
i can't find more
than momentary joy
i'm stuck in grief
the weight of it
in my chest
never-ending
my one release
alcohol
i know it's not
a healthy choice
but i reach
the point at which
i cannot bear
the pain another day

Memories
December 21, 2016

memories
floating bits of life
wandering in and out
providing hints
of life lived
evoked by music
or by smells
random sparks
some memories come
in whole pieces
a perfect picture
with all the senses
remembering
some memories come
in flashes barely
able to be contained
in a thought
elusive
hard to pin down
my life?
or another?

One Step At A Time
January 2, 2017

I made it through
the holidays
and into the new year.
I simply locked
my heart and tears
and forged a grim way through.
They caught up with me
more than once
preparing the table
thinking he should be there
listening to the Christmas tunes
knowing how he loved them.
But now it is
another year.
In truth I can
move through my days
while thoughts of him
come flitting in
not inevitably causing
grief to pull me down.
I'm learning to move on
to live anyway.
I've finally accepted that
he's on the other side.
I need to rediscover living

and I'm doing that
one
step
at
a
time.

Crossing A Line
January 3, 2017

I've crossed a line
the line between
2016 and 2017.
It's an arbitrary step
whose meaning comes
from ritual.
Last year was a big year.
I started writing
which led me on
a deep dive
into my past
into sexual abuse
and pain.
At the same time
unbeknownst to me
my son was on his
own deep dive
one he wouldn't survive.
There were moments
when I wondered
if what I felt
was all mine
or some part of his story.
It was only in looking back
I could see connections.
Overwhelmed with grief
Tom and I moved forward
with our wedding.

Afterward
I let the grief
have full rein on my being.
Now on the other side
of that annual line
I can feel a change.
It's now something in the past
not my every waking moment.
It doesn't mean that I don't cry
or yearn for more time with my son
but it no longer overwhelms me.
and I'm ready to resume my life
start caring for myself
start finding what new joys
that this new year will hold.

Ice Storm
January 8, 2017

Another ice storm.
The trees hang heavy
with the weight.
Trunks and limbs
lean to and fro
more potential
for heavy breakage.
Frozen emotions
come to mind
the weight of which
hang heavy in my heart
threatening to
break it suddenly.
Allowing them to melt
softening the pain
lets it flow away
leaving tenderness
in its warming wake.
Stormy days
a good time
to let it be.

Another Year
January 16, 2017

Another year
the same feelings
have come around
for another visit
antsy jitters
chest tight
can barely sit still
in my chair.
But I'm here.
I'm writing now
and I'll keep writing
if it keeps
the monsters from
devouring me
if it keeps me
clear and sane
I'll pay homage
to the Muse.
She tugs the sleeve
of my shirt
taps on the insides
of my eyelids
scratches on
the surface of
my mind
awaking dreams.
I could ignore her
scream somewhere

or take a walk
in the snow
or start drinking
after breakfast.
But it wouldn't
drive her off.
She has a purpose
I must follow.
I can't see more
of the path
than what's right
in front of me.
There's no obvious
direction;
the line is not
clear-cut.
It's just a journey
in the dark
blindly following
her lead.
Okay, I'll follow.
Let's go see
what treasure
we may find
along the way.

Photo by Jason

An Evening of Remembrance
January 17, 2017

Gathered round the dinner table
sharing stories with Jason's
best friend from high school
another one who adored him.
Once again I'm back to why.
I reach a point of acceptance
letting go and moving on.
Then something happens to bring back
the senselessness of loss.
That darkness that he hid so well
the one that ate at him
the one we glimpsed for years as he
did battle with depression.
How can someone sweet and good
so loving and so giving
not see what was clear to all of us?
How could he end it all?
It's hard to imagine
the depths of darkness
and despair
the pain, with death
the only seeming answer.

The bigger question is
what do I do from here?
Hide myself away?
Live a simple life?
Wander amongst the plants
that are my healing balm?

It's the thing you can't discuss
that can kill you
that dark passenger*
the thing you hold inside
the one you'll never tell a soul
they would be horrified
they'd hate you
disapprove.
You know it from the inside.
You know too well that thing.
But how do you find someone to tell
some place safe to unload?
So you move on
all the while
carrying the dark passenger
hoping, praying
that no one will ever know
no one will ever see
the truth of who you are.

And when the possibility
of exposure rears its head
you can face up
or you can die.

The term "dark passenger" is from the television series, Dexter. Jason loved the series and I've been watching – trying to understand, trying to connect.

Photo by Jason

Spring's Stirring
January 23, 2017

I'm trying to move.
The sadness continues to be
my constant companion.
My mind is a constant swirl.
I can feel the stirring of spring
the pressure of tasks
long left undone.
I no longer want to just curl up
in front of the fire
or stay in my cave
ignoring the rest of the world.
But I don't seem to have
any forward-moving energy.
So I'm letting it be
finding one thing
that calls me at the moment.
Baby steps they call it
steps into the now.
It seems insane
to keep a list of lists of lists
but somehow it makes all this
doing nothing be okay.
Things won't get lost.
But soon
I'll need to move.
Spring will be upon us
the busy time for work
for garden, plants and nature.

I'm counting on
the stirring of the spring
the quickening of nature
within my injured being
to burst this cloud of sadness
and carry me
to life again.

Your Presence
February 5, 2017

Your presence
engulfs my being.
I can feel you
as close as my breath.
You could be sitting
right here with me
engaged in conversation
or enjoying common space.
You've filled my mind
growing stronger every day
until today I know that you
are here, you're here with me.
Do you have a need?
Or are you helping
me to heal
from the pain and loss?
I only know I miss you daily.
I miss your smile
and your humor
and the warmth
of your presence.
Be well, my son.

Photo by (Unknown)

The Spaces Between
February 13, 2017

I haven't written in a while.
I've been wandering in the dark
hiding round the corner.
But now with spring upon us
I crawl up from the deepness
of the dark, moist Earth
and begin again.
There are bright days now.
The grief is not
always engulfing me
there are spaces in between
where I can breathe
enjoying life
where I can do and be
something more
it isn't always
full of hopeless tears
though they can still
catch me by surprise.
There are days filled with grief
but more are filled
with life and love
and possibility.
I still miss my son
his light, his smile, his humor
but I can now appreciate
the beauty in my life.

I'm learning
to embrace the living
and tuck my dearest son
into a quiet space
inside my heart.

The Darkness Surrounds Me
February 20, 2017

The darkness surrounds me
pressing in upon my being.
The tears no longer wash me clean.
They are dredging gullies in my soul
down deep into the earth of my being
baring stones of old hurts
crumbling away the stories
leaving me barren and empty.
I have nothing left to give
no love in my heart
no generosity in spirit
only deep, dark pain
that tears me limb from limb.
I lie fragmented in darkness
seeming lifeless
hopeless.
I have surrendered
given in to grief.
I am no more.

Photo by Jason

Returning to the Light
March 3, 2017

I awaken
I am here
I have my life
I have my family
I have my voice
My voice will save me
It will speak
Steer me back to love
It's an opening
The answer to my grief
Writing, sharing
Bringing forth new life
Returning me to the light.

Photo by Jason

A Gathering of Family
March 6, 2017

A gathering of family
honoring the birthday
of a loved one, now gone.
Candles fluttering
or flickering out in the breeze.
Flowers placed on the mandala
at his final resting place.
Bits of sharing
a few tears
some silence
some laughter.
Then on to a glass of wine,
a "blech" by Grandma as
she tastes the brew she doesn't like.
All in celebration of
the one we love and miss
who chose suicide
and left us with the pieces
of his shattered life.
There's no anger
just the missing
every day.
And learning to
remember humor
right along with pain.
As my daughter said
"He'd be angry if we wallowed."
So we celebrate and eat

spend lovely family time together.
One more step
in the wheel of the year
as the pain slowly fades
into the past.
We learn to stand
strong in the present
and await
a new future.

Happy Birthday
March 7, 2017

I sit here expectantly
waiting.
For what
I can't figure out.
Then I realize
it's for you,
so we can celebrate
your day.
But you're not here.
You won't be coming.
And the tears start to flow
and the skies cry along.
I miss you
my beautiful son.

Photo by Jason's father, Jason's sister Amber and Jason

Spring Forth
March 10, 2017

Movement
awakening and stretching
as if from a long nap.
Spring is here.
The air feels different.
The birds
oh my goodness, the birds
singing their sweet songs
pulling forth the life
from within my being.
Hello, spring.

Grief Sucks
March 18, 2017

It's right there again
all the angst and worry
the emotions
when I knew
Jason was in trouble
the sick feeling in my gut
the tension in my chest
the anxiety.
And it's not real.

I realize I'm different.
"Why" has always
been my question.
I've driven others nuts with it.
Why, what are you doing?
Why are you doing it?
It's what keeps me interested
finding reasons.

But the reasons are all gone.
Jason is gone.
There are no answers
to be found.
It's all over.
Why can't I let it go?

What's inside my head
rolling around

in the middle of the night
keeping me awake
giving me this anxious feeling?

Grief sucks.

A Window in Time
March 23, 2017

Drifting into the past
thinking about our last home
and the lovely gardens.
I remember saying goodbye
to the garden as we prepared
to leave for the last time.
I remember the tears
of farewell to the garden
a place of labor and joy
and a respite from the world.
And then I remember
the tears of farewell
I continue to cry for my son
and the tears start to flow.
That home was where
I'd raised my children
for their middle
and high school years.
It's where I'd sent them off into
the world to make their lives.
Looking back on saying
goodbye to the garden
is like a window in time
before Jason's death
and the pain since.
I had no idea
as we set off on
our new home adventure

of what was yet to come.
A strange set of emotions
to mix in my mind.

Dispelling the Energy
April 18, 2017

feeling stressed
mind buzzing
bits of Jason
floating through
my day
back to this
task or that
frantic feeling
must
go
do
something
to dispel
this energy

His Civic Nature
March 27, 2017

Driving down the road
I see new construction
at the business park
near where Jason worked.
Or...
Going to visit family
the road is all torn up
construction in full force.
Or...
I read an article about
a brand-new restaurant
being built along the river.
And...
I think to myself
if Jason were still alive
I'd know all about these
before I even saw them.
He'd have let us know
about the road construction
anything that might disturb our day.
That's how he was.
He loved to track these projects
road construction
building ventures
around the county.
It was part of his civic nature.
Another piece missed
and a few more tears shed.

Photo by Matthew Bernard Bentson-Royal

Standing in the Midst
March 29, 2017

I stand in the midst
of your life and mine.
I feel this deep ache
in my heart and my soul.
Is it my own
or is it yours
flung across the great divide
pining for the life you chose
to let go?

Photo by Matthew Bernard Bentson-Royal

What Does Today Hold
March 31, 2017

I've been contemplating grief recently. I have experienced grief since my son's death last July. I've reached that stage where it seems I should move on. And I have. But...

Grief is an interesting mind state. There are times when it completely engulfs me and my day. I have learned over these months to keep moving, go on living my life. I carry the grief with me throughout the day. It's like grief has replaced the child I no longer have.

When my son was a baby, I carried him. When he was old enough to carry himself physically, I still carried him in my heart. After his first suicide attempt at age 21, that changed. I not only held him in my heart, but I also fought hard to hold him on this Earth. I probably didn't have all the best tools, but dammit, I tried.

For twelve years, I held him so close to me. He grew and matured. But on occasion, he'd attempt suicide again. It seemed there was nothing I could do but love him. And for a while, that held him here. But then he was gone. Now I carry grief in my heart the same way I used to carry him as a baby, and like the worry for him I carried throughout his life.

Most days now, I think of him in passing and go

on with my day. But some days…

No Do-Overs
April 5, 2017

Jason's picture sits in my office. I placed it low on a bookcase for his cat, Mr. Kitty, who now lives with us. When I had the picture up high, Mr. Kitty was always climbing – on the piano, on a bookcase, wherever that picture was. So I moved it down low where he could see it, and it helped. But I see it every day as I move around my home office. The seeing inspired this poem.

Hold on?
Turn my back.
Pretend it's not there.
Look him straight in the eye.
Stay busy.
Look forward
all the time
carrying the anguish.
It's the way of life
when you've lost
a loved one to suicide.
There are no do-overs.
There are no answers.
It simply is.
He passed the torch
now I get to carry the pain.
It's not what he would have wanted
but I just
can't
make it go away.

The worry
has been replaced
by grief.

Breaking Down Barriers
April 12, 2017

Breaking down barriers
dredging through the mind
finding ways to cope
building a life to be proud of.
It's never easy to make a change.
I want to run away
I want life to be easy
I suppose that would be boring.
So I look forward
I take the step in front of me.
I walk along this pathway
wandering in the forest
of my mind
knowing
I can make it through
to the other side
and feel the joy again.

Photo by Jason

The Man Behind the Beautiful Mask
April 19, 2017

shift
heavy
wandering
can't
quite
grasp
onto my day.

I've been reading
Jason's journal.

He was lonely.
He wasn't good at relationships.
He wanted a special person in his life
almost more than anything.
He buried his pain in alcohol.
He wanted to be held.
A few times he alludes to his
not being good in bed.
He talks about how hooking up
makes him loathe himself
yet as the years went on
he hooked up more and more
less risk to his heart, I guess
than a real relationship
but making one less likely.
It turns out there were four attempts
he made upon his life

but with the first he went to sleep
and woke up the next day
so no one ever knew.
At times he loved to be with family
at others not so much.
It seems that he did lots of things
under pressure from his peers.
I guess that also added to
his loathing for himself.
He was obsessed with
thoughts of cleaning
exercising, eating healthy
things he seldom actually
followed through on.
And his money was a mess.
When he died
though making good money
he left behind a pile of bills.

Good Mom?
April 19, 2017

They said I was
a good mom.
I'm not so sure
anymore.
I think I had
a lot of failings
that colored the world
of my children's minds.
For years we all
kept up the story
but things began
to crumble.
One child now
is blossoming into
an amazing woman
but she's fought
to become who she is.
It's been her journey
and I'm not sure
how much a hand
I had in it.

I guess that this
is rock bottom.
Who I am
and how I lived
may have killed
my son.

So where to from here?

Ponderings on Life Without Jason
May 1, 2017

This weekend I had such a feeling of gratitude for my life as it is today. I have a wonderful husband and family. I find beauty in so much of our home as we work to make it ours. And then I remembered Jason. The guilt wanted to insert itself into the moment. I turned back to gratitude.

Later, Tom and I were sitting at the picnic table looking at our deck building project—very much in the beginning stages. Our old dog, Hans, wanted to be held. It's a bit challenging holding a dog while sitting at a picnic table, but I gave in and picked him up. I said something to the effect of, "When did I get so soft?" And the memory catches my breath and brings tears to my eyes. "I should have held him more," plays in my mind. It's been almost a mantra in my mind since Jason's death. I breathe through the pain and return to the moment.

This morning, I realize I need to shift my relationship to Jason. The challenge is to not carry the burden of his failed life as my own. I want to forgive myself for any failings I may have had as a parent that contributed to his mental illness. The rest is his. And I want to remember still the best of who he was. I want the wonderful memories. But I need to find a way not to make everything about Jason.

A Nighttime Visit
May 4, 2017

Jason has been in my dreams
the last few nights.
They've been pleasant bits
of meals shared and
time spent together.
It's been many weeks
since he's ventured into
the dreamscape of my mind.
The difference now —
I awaken
and enjoy
the beauty of the dream.
The grief stays way
in the background
like a soft cloud on
a summer afternoon.
Tom and I share stories
about funny things
Jason might have
said or done
with just the slightest tinge
of the grief that once
seemed to engulf me.
I don't know if this
is permanent
or a temporary passing.
But for now
I'll take the change.

This Roller Coaster Called Grief
May 5, 2017

one moment
enjoying memories
a wonderful chat
with my daughter
about moving on
then a song plays
and the tears
start to fall
funny thing
the song has no
relation to Jason
just somehow touches
the emotions
floating on the surface

Photo by Jason

Driving Down the Road
May 10, 2017

Driving down the road
music in the background
the sound of the tires
on the pavement
eyes wandering
enjoying the ride.
I start to feel you
your emotions
your thoughts.
I think about
the night you died
the way it might
have played out.
Did you have
any regrets
as your breath ran out?
I think of the weeks
leading up to your death.
I can almost feel
the desperation
the self-loathing
the disappointments
of your life
the love that you
could never find
the frustrations
with yourself.
The tears begin to fall.

I feel caught between
your lost life
and mine.
I just let it roll
as I wander down the road.
Eventually
the tears fade
and it's as though
you're riding there
next to me in the car
like so many other
trips we took
time shared
with no need for words.

Warm Day Memories
May 10, 2017

As the summer sun returns
the cool, crisp mornings cede
to warm afternoons.
The trees are full in green glory.
Flowers fill the landscape.
I wear your sweatshirt, that gray one
I watched you wearing as you worked
on the hillside pathway.
It keeps me warm as I work
on today's tasks.
I remember the times
that we wandered along
enjoying our new home
looking for the borders
trimming up the trees
just enjoying time together.
We miss you often.
You are forever woven
into our loving home.

Photo by Jason

Mother's Day, Part 1
May 14, 2017
My Facebook post @ 9:53 am

I woke this morning
heard a text come in
wishing me
Happy Mother's Day
from my daughter-in-law
Marie.
I went back to bed.
Ten minutes later
I heard this horrible noise.
I got up
went out to find
the Roomba spinning
in circles.
Tom later said
it must be Jason
wishing me
a Happy Mother's Day —
I guess not wanting
to be outdone
by Marie.

Mother's Day, Part 2
May 14, 2017
A few hours later

Another holiday
Mother's Day
and the rain drones on.
Early morning loves
from my daughter
and daughter-in-law.
Fun making a meme
to celebrate my mom.
A flippant comment
by my loving husband,
"You're not my mother"
and down the rabbit hole
I go.
Tears start to fall
into the breakfast
I'm preparing.
Words become
impossible.
Jason always
came to spend
this day with me.
Perhaps we'd go to breakfast
or he'd help me with
a garden project or two.
Time spent
in gentle loving.
Those days are gone

and I find myself
back in the grief
one more time.

Mother's Day, Part 3
May 14, 2017
Another Facebook post @ 9:15 pm

Last story
of this Mother's Day.
We sat down
to watch a movie.
I looked out the window
saw some extra colors.
When I went out
I found this balloon
hanging from
the dogwood tree.
The message says,
"I miss you, Mom.
Love you very much.
Always thinking of you."

Photo by Victoria

Mr. Kitty's Freedom
May 27, 2017

It's a beautiful summer's evening.
I guess more accurately it's spring
but the warmth in the air
makes it feel like summer.
Tom's music in the background
chickens running around, nibbling.
Mr. Kitty wanders down the lane
going who knows where.
Mr. Kitty was Jason's cat.
He spent his first eight years
as an apartment cat
safe and secure
viewing the world from the comfort
of his fifth-floor deck.
Once Jason's life began unraveling
he and Mr. Kitty
came to stay.
After Jason's suicide
we made the decision
Mr. Kitty would receive
the same freedom
as our other cat, Nelson.
I'm sure that there are those
who'd say we're irresponsible.
You see, we live in the woods
surrounded by wild things
like coyote, bobcat, fox, and bear.
But watching Mr. Kitty

tripping down the lane
or pouncing in the grass
searching for a mouse
I'm not so sure.
As a parent, you do all
in your power to protect
your children.
But in the end
it's not in your hands.
They get to make their own decisions.
I watched as Jason made his.
I knew the risks—
he'd tried it before.
So now, we allow
Mr. Kitty all his freedom.
If there's anything I've learned
I can't protect him
from Life.

He Knew
June 1, 2017

Memories.
A glimpse of a moment in time.
He stood there in the doorway
saying goodbye.
He knew, but I didn't
It would be the last time.

We'd spent the morning
working on computer problems.
He'd taken a shower
was prepared to leave.
I don't recall his exact words.
Did he say
Goodbye
See ya
Have a nice weekend?
I'm not sure.
He hesitated
then turned and walked through the door
for the last time
knowing what he was about to do.
Today, I'm angry.
He knew, but I didn't.
I could have given him a hug.
But I didn't.
It echoes again.
I should have held him more.
Would it have made a difference?

Likely not
because he knew
and I didn't.

Photo by Jason

Moving Forward
June 12, 2017

The pain is dulled now
it's no longer sharp
no longer takes my breath away
it's a heavy reminder
I carry 'round from day to day
the knowing that he's gone
the senselessness of it all
my seeming failure as a parent.
His death is not my fault.
He made a choice.
He followed through
made sure this time.
Here we are.
Life is moving forward
there's no choice.
But he's on my mind today.
We're in the shadow of the day.
It was during this time last year
that he was living with us.
I knew every day he left
he might not come back.
We knew this could happen.
But, dammit! The aftermath.
It's tough moving on.
It's tough letting go.
There's a piece of me
that would like to erase him
from our home.

Then I wouldn't see the pictures.
I wouldn't remember every day
he's gone.
I'm pretty sure that's not true.
And Mr. Kitty might miss his picture.
I watch him, wondering.
Does he remember?
Does he miss his old life?
Does he miss his Person?
I think Mr. Kitty
likes his new life better
lots of space and freedom.
But what about his Person
what about my son?
For now Mr. Kitty and I
get to love on one another
and move forward together.

Black and White and Tuna Sandwiches
June 22, 2017

He always drew lines —
it was black
or it was white
no allowance for life.
Age five —
I'm making tuna sandwiches.
He tells me that I did it wrong.
How can it be wrong?
I should have made them
the way his daycare
provider made them
that's how you make sandwiches.
In the last few years
the black and white lines
started turning gray.
I thought he was progressing.
I thought he was maturing.
We can't always know
what is right or wrong
for another person.
Losing black and white
put him at the edge.
Those lines of black and white
provided him with safety
kept him on the good side.
And in the end
the line's loss
led him to his death.

Photo by Jason

Choice Points
June 27, 2017

choice points
those moments
every day
live or die
care for self
throw it all away
forge ahead
give it up
create beauty
hate the world
check that phone
one more time
look deeply
into the eyes
of the person
in front of me
discipline
love and nurture
be right
be kind
self-loathing
forgiveness
do that thing
stay the course
wait it out
step off the edge
choices
every day

what do you choose
please choose Life

In memory of one who didn't

Photo by Jason

A Frame of Photos
June 28, 2017

A frame of photos
hangs on the wall
a gift from my daughter
from a former time.
The image of Jason
was an odd one
one I never liked.
But after his suicide
the scruffy beard
leather jacket
and sorrowful look
seemed more
connected to
his final days
than to life.
Tom said
it needed to go
and I agreed.
It's been on my list
of things to do
ever since.
Today
I replaced the picture.
I made other changes
because life moves on.
My grandson graduated.
My daughter's family has changed.
All markers of time.

Making all the changes
required I look back
over the past in photos.
That usually brings tears.
But today
I got the job done.
I checked the task complete.
Ah, here come
the expected tears.
One more step
checked off
of a life
no longer with us.

Coming Home
June 6, 2017

I realize
I'm coming home
to myself.
That's not
necessarily
a good thing.
After Jason's death
all that I could feel
was grief.
It came in many forms
but always there.
Now
I'm starting to feel
all my old feelings
the things that used
to haunt me in
the middle of the night
my failings and
the places where I'm less.
It's all back
and somehow
it feels worse.
I realize my demons
became my son's
the weight of which
he couldn't bear.
And now I must bear
not only my failings

but the loss
of my son.
It's a heavy load.
And today
it's almost unbearable.

Almost a Year
July 6, 2017

You left us
almost a year ago.
This book is coming to an end
but the journey goes on.
I'm beginning to realize
there is no end to grief.
My breath catches less.
The weight has grown more bearable.
We can laugh at your antics
or things we remember
though the pain
still rides deep within
cutting into the joy.
My advice to others—
hold on.
It doesn't get much easier
but it becomes tolerable.
One day
you will find
that you've found your old life.
It's returned to you
colored a little differently.
And yes
there will still be pain
the tears will still erupt
unbidden.
But love remains.
And time really does heal.

We can survive.

Photo by Amber (Jason's sister)

Some Things
July 11, 2017

Some things
are never forgiven.
They are the moments
I should have loved
instead of disciplined
the harsh words
instead of gentle.
It's time I spent
chasing dreams
careers
great advances
when time
with my children
may have saved a life.
I must go on
learn to live
with the knowing
that perhaps
just perhaps
those things
might have changed
the outcome
of my son's life.
Forgiveness?
No
it's best to hold on
remember
and learn.

In a Different Reality
July 12, 2017

In a different reality
you'd be living in
that luxury condo I passed
coming home from town today.
In a different reality
you'd have found your person
the one who makes your heart sing
who loves you to the moon and back.
In a different reality
you'd have married your person
maybe had a family.
I know there'd be no picket fences
'cause that's not your style.
In a different reality
you'd have shone in your work
and in your private life.
In a different reality
depression and self-loathing
wouldn't have been your companions.
In a different reality
you'd still be here with us.

I Was a Tormented Soul
July 1, 2017

These words came from his heart through mine as a closing poem.

I was a tormented soul
drowning alone in the dark.
I couldn't share with you
the depths of pain in my heart.
I was terrified
of the places my mind went
of feelings I couldn't control.
I wanted release from suffering
to find peace and comfort.
I wanted someone to love
and to be loved in return.
I wanted to feel good
about the man I was.
I didn't want to feel alone.
I loved you all--
my family, friends, and co-workers.
You were what kept me here
for as long as I stayed.
But in the end
the dark outweighed the light.
I could no longer fight
the demons inside.
I know you loved me
even at this great cost.
I will always love you.

Photo by Victoria, the path referred to in this book

Epilogue
What is Grief Like?

Each person processes grief in their own way. For some, it's an internal affair. No one ever knows the person is grieving. From the outside, it can appear the person is ignoring what has happened and simply moving on with life. For some, this is in fact what they are doing. The grief may or may not come back later in the form of physical ailments or emotional issues seemingly unrelated to the original grief. Others simply suffer in silence.

Some people process their grief more publicly, allowing their tears to fall when they arise. I was one of these people. For the first month after Jason's death, I was incredibly busy. We had a Celebration of Life to prepare for and then our wedding three weeks later. I threw myself into preparations, yard work, whatever was at hand to keep me busy. I was almost manic in my actions. The tears flowed as I worked, but I kept moving. And once the wedding was over and family had gone home, I stopped.

I simply allowed myself to float. I didn't have to do anything besides the basics of daily life. The garden could wait. The paint I'd purchased at the beginning of summer to paint the living room could stay in the can. I didn't have to exercise or do anything unnecessary. I did a lot of walking around our property, crying, remembering and trying to figure it all out.

I can't say I used the best of coping skills regarding Jason's death. I drank too much alcohol and lost far too many hours watching movies and television. I ate all the comfort food I wanted, though at times I had no appetite. I was silent and unavailable at times to those I love who are still living. I did the best I could with relationships.

I have always been a deeply spiritual person but found myself unable to connect to my spiritual center. I would sit down to meditate, and the tears would start to roll. I started avoiding anything related to spirituality. I wasn't angry with God; I just couldn't feel anything. I wasn't ready.

Poetry has been my best coping skill. It has given me a tool to express the depths of my grief, allowing me at least momentary respite.

In the weeks and months after his death, the poetry likely saved my life. It gave me an outlet for the many hours of gut-wrenching soul-searching I did regarding Jason's life and death. I spent sleepless nights thinking about his last minutes. Did he panic? Did he wish he had taken a different path? Was he surprised to cross over and find it wasn't all over with but now a new journey to healing was in order?

I hacked into Jason's world. I trawled through his computer looking at every picture, watching every video, and reading emails. I listened to his music and watched his movies. In time, I even binge-watched one of his favorite television shows, *Dexter*. It seemed if I could just get inside his head enough, I'd understand. I think some part of me thought I could bring him back if I could find the key.

But there were no definitive answers. Each time I seemed to find answers, I also found more questions. I started to write a book of Jason's life story, filling it with every memory I had of him. It became another obsession, stirring the details around and around trying to find the best order. And trying to find the answers. In time, I realized this too was part of my grieving process. It was a way to try and hold him close, to not let him go.

I realized I had to start letting go. I put the book away. I closed Jason's computer and started trying to pick up the pieces of my life.

It's hard. There is no right way to grieve. There are no signposts to say you are on the right path so you have to put one foot in front of the other and keep moving. Writing helped to give my mind an outlet. And in time I started finding solace in some of the things I loved before Jason's death.

If I were to give anyone advice on how to cope with the suicide of a loved one, I'd urge you to find a creative outlet. Make art out of your grief. Write, paint, sculpt, weld, garden, make music, volunteer. It doesn't have to be good; it just has to give your heart and mind an outlet.

It will still hurt. Tears will still come at will. Life will still be hard. But at least you'll have something concrete to lead you forward.

If someone you know has lost a loved one to suicide, just be there. Hold them, love them, listen to them. Tell them you're sorry. There's nothing more you need to do. Being there will be enough.

Was there something more or different I could have done? Was there something I missed I should have seen? Here's what I believe to be true. When I look back at my son's life, I see it from my perspective. I can see all the good, and though I know the darkness sometimes clouded it for him, for me, the good is what I remember. Who my son was at his best makes the last few months of his life and the final ending, all seem so senseless. And then I remember—depression colored his vision.

The National Institute of Mental Health states, "Depression is a common but serious mood disorder. It causes severe symptoms that affect how you feel, think, and handle daily activities.[1]" A person suffering from depression sees the world differently. I can't look at his life and understand how he got to suicide because I don't see the world the same way he did.

I believe there were three elements that led to

---

[1] The National Institute of Mental Health. (2016, October). Depression. Retrieved March 2, 2017, from https://www.nimh.nih.gov/health/topics/depression/index.shtml

Jason's final decision. First, when I look at his life, I know he felt alone. He was 33 at the time of his death and he had been unable to form a lasting significant relationship. He had tried living with roommates but found that difficult. But then he struggled with living alone and attributed it to being a factor in at least two of his previous suicide attempts.

I feel sad when I think of how my son felt so alone in this world. We normally connected on a weekly basis, but that is a few hours out of a long week when a person is depressed and lonely.

The second element was how he dealt with his emotional challenges. It seems he never developed tools to handle difficult emotions. Whenever his life got really difficult, he'd attempt suicide.

Jason tried four previous times to take his life starting at age 21. The first time he took too many pills, fell asleep and woke the next day. No one even knew until I read his journal after his death.

Each of the other times, he called 911 before passing out. They took him to the hospital, and he worked with staff to choose a treatment route. Unfortunately, after the first hospitalization, they focused his treatment on alcohol and marijuana use. The mental illness and the inner turmoil causing him to choose suicide weren't addressed. And, with each attempt, he was getting closer to success.

It seemed he made some progress when he

checked himself into the hospital about sixteen months before his death. Once he got out, he felt he had a plan. And it worked for a little while. He had several significant challenges and seemed to handle them. But then things started shifting. In looking back, I realize his moods got darker. He wasn't quite as well-kempt. His visits got longer, but it wasn't like there was a real purpose. He just sat in a chair.

The final element was the loss of his job a few weeks before his death. Jason took great pride in his work. It was a big part of who he was and helped compensate for his lack of a significant person in his life. The loss of his job combined with the trouble he got himself into likely caused him to feel worthless, a burden on others. His life was adrift, and there was no clear path to a workable end.

I had two different conversations with the detective who investigated Jason's death. She told me that, in her experience, there was nothing we could have done. When a person decides to take their life, there is little that others can do change it. I don't know if I agree with her in all cases. But in this case, I think she was right. We could have had him committed or chained him to our home. But in the end, he would have found a way out.

Her other advice was to honor my son's life by raising the bar in my life. I could take all the good that was in Jason's life and create something special.

We live in a culture where it can seem we are expected to grieve in private and get on with it. But we need to know we are not alone. We need to know it's okay to grieve and that grief doesn't feel a particular way or go away on a timeline.

This poetry helped me to deal with my grief, and putting it into a book seemed an obvious next step. There have been times in working on this book that I have sensed Jason's support. Whether it was inspiration for solving a technical issue or pointing out something that needed changing or that song he loved playing on the radio, I know he approves. If this book can help another parent find their footing in this world called grief, I will have made a difference.

Author Bio

Victoria Polmatier is best known for her loving heart and laughter. She's happiest when sharing time with family or writing a poem about life or when she has her hands in the dirt tending her herbs and garden. Victoria lives in Southwest Washington with her husband, their two dogs, two cats and a flock of chickens. She can be found on social media as "naturalvic" or her website at www.victoriapolmatier.com.

www.ingramcontent.com/pod-product-compliance
Lightning Source LLC
Chambersburg PA
CBHW040334300426
44113CB00021B/2749